Little

Growing the Fruit of the Spirit

tate publishing
CHILDREN'S DIVISION

Holly M. Roddam

Published by Tate Publishing & Enterprises, LLC
127 E. Trade Center Terrace | Mustang, Oklahoma 73064 USA
1.888.361.9473 | www.tatepublishing.com

Tate Publishing is committed to excellence in the publishing industry. The company reflects the philosophy established by the founders, based on Psalm 68:11,
"The Lord gave the word and great was the company of those who published it."

Book design copyright © 2014 by Tate Publishing, LLC. All rights reserved.
Cover and interior design by Errol Villamante
Illustrations by Patrick Bucoy

Published in the United States of America

ISBN: 978-1-63063-352-3
Juvenile Nonfiction / Religion / Christianity
14.01.31

Dedicated to Mikayla and Dylan, two bright cities on a hill shining for Jesus. May the Fruit of the Spirit continue to grow in you all the days of your lives.

Love, Nana xoxo

I'm a Little Child of God

And so I want to be

A light that shines in darkness

For all the world to see.

Jesus said to take my light

And let it shine for Him

A city on top of a big, big hill,

So my light would not be dim!

How do I let my little Light shine?

How do I let it show?

By letting God's Spirit live in me

So the Fruit of the Spirit will grow!

Love is easy to give to those

On whom my life depends,

But when I love those who

are mean to me,

My love turns them into my friends!

Joy is the proof that

my faith is strong.

The Joy of the Lord makes me sing.

No matter what happens or

where my path leads,

Joy leads me to Jesus, my King.

Peace says, "I don't have to be afraid!"

When I ask Holy Spirit to guide.

Though storms may come,

the safest place

Is with Jesus at my side.

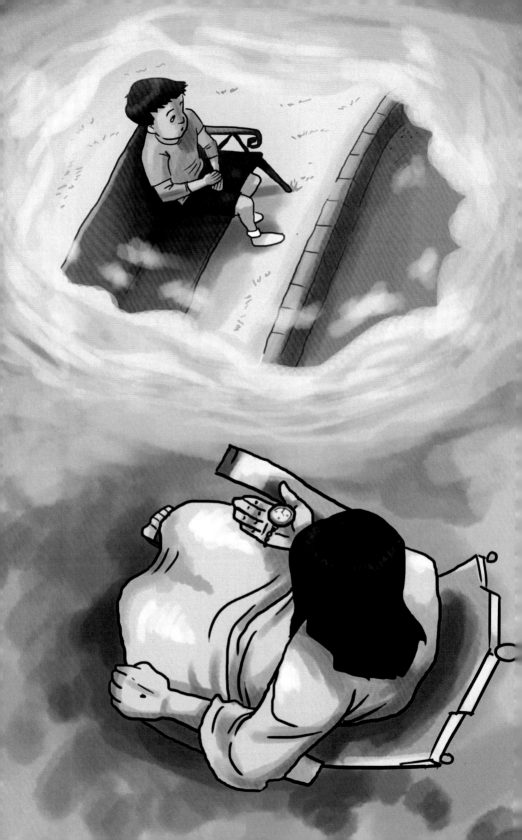

Patience shows when things don't go
The way I want them to,
And I quietly wait for the perfect time
For God's promises to come true.

Kindness is seen in the little things

That I do when others are near;

Like sharing my toys and

not playing rough,

Or wiping away someone's tear.

Goodness is special

because God is good,

All the time and in every way.

When I act like Him and

choose to be good,

Godly actions chase bad ones away!

Faithfulness means I keep my word
'Cause I know God's Word is true.
Jesus has always been faithful to me
So I want to be trustworthy too.

Gentleness, known as

Meekness sometimes,

Is important to understand.

You'll never go wrong if

you humble yourself

Or offer to lend a hand.

Self-control, prob'ly the hardest of all

But a Child of God needs this key!

Being guided by God's Holy Spirit

Grows the Fruit of the Spirit in me!

So if you see me doing my best

To be a bright light on the hill,

Please tell me I'm doing

a really good job,

And you know, I probably will!

Note From a Little Child of God

Mom and Dad, teachers and grown ups,
Please encourage me as I live for Jesus. If you point out
the things I do right, I'll do them again ☺. When I do
something wrong, please correct me with gentleness and
love. The Fruit of the Spirit is for grown-ups too ☺.

Thank you!

Take Time to Grow Some Fruit

Note to Parents and Teachers:

Read the story often so your child can learn the verses about the Fruit of the Spirit. Use these questions to discuss with your child what it means to grow the Fruit of the Spirit in his or her life. Adapt the ideas to suit your child's age.

Each scripture illustrates one of the fruits and the opening and closing verses. Focus on one at a time. Don't try to do too much at once, but help your child digest little bits at a time until it becomes part of their understanding. Have fun growing your fruit ☺.

The Fruit of the Spirit

But the Holy Spirit produces this kind of fruit in our lives: love, joy, peace, patience, kindness, goodness, faithfulness, gentleness, and self-control. There is no law against these things!

Galatians 5:22-23 (NLT)

1. What are the 9 Fruit of the Spirit?

    Memorize them in groups of 3:
    - Love, Joy, Peace
    - Patience, Kindness, Goodness
    - Faithfulness, Gentleness and Self-Control

2. Why is it good to grow this fruit in your life?

Being a Little Child of God

... become blameless and pure, children of God without fault in a crooked and depraved generation, in which you shine like stars in the universe as you hold out the word of life...

Phil 2:15-16a (NIV)

3. What do the words "blameless", "pure", "crooked" and "depraved" mean?

4. How can I "shine like a star"?

5. What is the "word of life"? How do I "hold it out"?

6. Do others see Fruit of the Spirit in my behavior and life?

Being the Light of the World

You are the light of the world—like a city on a hilltop that cannot be hidden. No one lights a lamp and then puts it under a basket. Instead, a lamp is placed on a stand, where it gives light to everyone in the house. In the same way, let your good deeds shine out for all to see, so that everyone will praise your heavenly Father.

Matthew 5:14-16 (NLT)

7. Why did Jesus call us the "light of the world"?

8. Sing "This Little Light of Mine" to remind yourself that you are to live in a way that brings Jesus' light to everyone you meet.

9. Am I letting my light shine so that people will see and praise God because of it?

How to Grow the Fruit of the Spirit

Respect and obey the LORD! This is the beginning of knowledge. Only a fool rejects wisdom and good advice. My child, obey the teachings of your parents, and wear their teachings as you would a lovely hat or a pretty necklace.

Proverbs 1:7-9 (CEV)

Everyone who has been wise will shine as bright as the sky above, and everyone who has led others to please God will shine like the stars.

Daniel 12:3 (CEV)

10. Am I being wise? Do I obey my parents and teachers?

11. Who can I tell about growing the Fruit of the Spirit so they can do it too?

12. Have I asked Jesus to forgive me for things I have done wrong?

13. Do I have a friend who needs to know Jesus? Tell your friend that Jesus loves them and wants to grow the Fruit of the Spirit in their life too.

14. Ask your friend if they want to pray this prayer with you:

Dear Jesus,

Thank you for dying on the cross to forgive me for all the things I have done wrong. Please come into my heart to live. Holy Spirit, I want your fruit to grow in my life so that people will see that you live in me. Please help me to grow up to be loving, joyful, peaceful and kind like you. I love you Jesus and want my friends to know you too. Thank you for loving me and being my Best Forever Friend.

Amen.

Love

Love is patient and kind. *Love* is not jealous, it does not brag, and it is not proud. *Love* is not rude, is not selfish, and does not get upset with others. *Love* does not count up wrongs that have been done. *Love* takes no pleasure in evil but rejoices over the truth. *Love* patiently accepts all things. It always trusts, always hopes, and always endures. So these three things continue forever: faith, hope, and love. And the greatest of these is love.

1 Corinthians 13:4-7, 13 (NCV)

15. Read this scripture passage and put your name in the verses every time you see the word "*Love*". Example: "Holly is patient and kind. Holly is not jealous…" Is it true? Are you patient and kind? This is a good way to tell if you have the fruit of Love growing in your heart.

Joy

The Lord is my strength and shield. I trust him with all my heart. He helps me, and my heart is filled with joy. I burst out in songs of thanksgiving.

Psalm 28:7 (NLT)

16. Am I happy and joyful? Do I catch myself singing joyful songs of love for Jesus?

17. Do I trust Jesus with all my heart? You have to know Him to trust Him. Ask someone to help you read about Him in the Gospels, the books of the Bible called Matthew, Mark, Luke and John. Get to know Jesus by reading about what He did and said when He was on earth.

18. Talk to Jesus. We call this prayer. Prayer is a conversation with God, so don't forget to listen and let Him talk back to you! Be sure to thank Him for all the good things He has given you and done for you.

Peace

Do not worry about anything, but pray and ask God for everything you need, always giving thanks. And God's peace, which is so great we cannot understand it, will keep your hearts and minds in Christ Jesus.

Philippians 4:6-7 (NCV)

19. When we pray and ask God to look after us, we can have peace because He is faithful to care for us and give us what we need. Tell Jesus if there are things you are worried about and ask Him if He will take care of those things for you. Then, don't worry, be peaceful – and happy ☺.

20. Thank Jesus for caring for you, even before you see how He is doing it or answering your prayers. When we have a thankful heart, it seems to speed His answers along and reminds us that He is working on it for us.

21. If you have a hard time giving something to Jesus that is bothering you, sit in a quiet place and put your hands on your knees. Turn your hands down like you are dropping something on the floor. Think about the problem and drop it out of your hands saying, "Jesus, I give you this problem. I trust You to take it and make it right." Then turn your hands up and say, "Thank you, Jesus, for your peace. Let it fill

me up from the tips of my fingers to the top of my head and all the way down to the bottom of my feet. I want my heart and mind to rest in your amazing peace. Amen."

Patience

... And the Scriptures give us hope and encouragement as we wait patiently for God's promises to be fulfilled. May God, who gives this patience and encouragement, help you live in complete harmony with each other, as is fitting for followers of Christ Jesus. Then all of you can join together with one voice, giving praise and glory to God, the Father of our Lord Jesus Christ.

Romans 15:4-6 (NLT)

22. Do I want my way all the time? Do I want things "RIGHT NOW!"? Ask a grown up to help you find some Bible verses to learn that will help you understand how patient God is and how He wants us to be like Him.

23. Read about Abraham and Sarah who waited for years to have a baby (Gen 18:1-15; Rom 4:18-25). Read about Joseph who was in prison for many years before God made him the ruler over all of Egypt (Gen 39-41). Read about Simeon and Anna in the Temple who waited to see Baby Jesus until they were old (Luke 2:22-40). There are lots of stories in the Bible about people who were patient until God's promises came true. When we see that God keeps His promises when the time is right, it will help us know that He will do the same for us, and we can patiently wait for His timing.

24. Do you know someone who is waiting for something? Maybe someone is waiting for a new baby to be born. Someone going on a trip might have to be patient until the day to leave comes. See if you can encourage them to be patient by waiting with them and sharing the excitement of their special event until it happens. Talk about how fun it will be to have a new brother or sister, or go on their trip. This can help us be patient because it reminds us that it will really happen when the time is right.

Kindness

He has been very kind and patient, waiting for you to change, but you think nothing of his kindness. Perhaps you do not understand that God is kind to you so you will change your hearts and lives. God will reward or punish every person for what that person has done. Some people, by always continuing to do good, live for God's glory, for honor, and for life that has no end. God will give them life forever.

Romans 2:4, 6-7 (NCV)

25. Did you know that God is patient with us? Sometimes we don't obey as quickly as we should, or we get busy and forget to talk to Him or sit and visit with Him. Sometimes we are being stubborn or mean and we don't want to change, but God patiently waits for us to hear and obey His Word. He is always kind and loving toward us, even if we don't deserve it, because He wants us to be like Jesus.

26. One day, we will meet Jesus face to face and He will reward us for how much good fruit we have in our lives. If we don't let His fruit grow in us, we will be punished. But if you ask Jesus to forgive you for

growing bad fruit He will forgive you. Ask Him to come into your heart to live, and grow the Fruit of the Spirit. Obey God's Word found in the Bible because it is better to get a reward and live with Jesus!

Goodness

By his divine power, God has given us everything we need for living a godly life. We have received all of this by coming to know Him, the one who called us to Himself by means of his marvelous glory and excellence. And because of his glory and excellence, he has given us great and precious promises. These are the promises that enable you to share his divine nature and escape the world's corruption caused by human desires.

2 Peter 1:3-4 (NLT)

27. Reading the Bible is very important because it tells us how we can be like Jesus. He gives us the Holy Spirit to live in our heart and teach us how to be like Him. Holy Spirit also gives us the power to walk in obedience. What is your favorite Bible promise? Memorize it and say it often.

28. The Bible also tells us all the things God promises will be ours when we become His Child. If you are a Little Child of God, you will receive the same gifts and blessings that Jesus received. We are "heirs" with Jesus, because we are His brothers and sisters. If you don't have a Bible, ask for one for your birthday or Easter or Christmas, or just because you want to learn what God's promises are to you.

Faithfulness

The faithful love of the Lord never ends! His mercies never cease. Great is his faithfulness; his mercies begin afresh each morning. I say to myself, "The Lord is my inheritance; therefore, I will hope in Him!"

Lamentations 3:22-24 (NLT)

29. The Lord is always faithful. He wants us to be faithful too. Jesus said, "Let your 'yes' be 'yes' and your 'no' be 'no'." What does this mean?

30. What is an "inheritance"? How is Jesus our inheritance?

Gentleness

"When you are invited to a wedding feast, don't sit in the seat of honor. What if someone who is more distinguished than you has also been invited? The host will come and say, 'Give this person your seat.' Then you will be embarrassed, and you will have to take whatever seat is left at the foot of the table! Instead, take the lowest place at the foot of the table. Then when your host sees you, he will come and say, 'Friend, we have a better place for you!' Then you will be honored in front of all the other guests. For those who exalt themselves will be humbled, and those who humble themselves will be exalted."

Luke 14:8-11 (NLT)

31. What does it mean to be humble? If you always take the best seat are you being humble?

32. Sometimes people think the word "meekness" means that you are wimpy or that people can walk all over you. Meekness is a very strong word, the

opposite of being wimpy! It means God-fearing, righteous, humble, teachable, and patient when you are suffering. It is having the power to do harm to someone, but choosing to follow Jesus' teachings and do good instead. It is a characteristic of a true Child of God.

33. If you try to make yourself more important than everyone else, people will want to knock you down. Being gentle and humble shows you are meek – you may have the ability to put yourself ahead of others, but you choose to put others ahead of yourself. Then people will want to praise you and lift you up.

Self-control

For the grace of God that brings salvation has appeared to all men. It teaches us to say "No" to ungodliness and worldly passions, and to live self-controlled, upright and godly lives in this present age.

Titus 2:11-12 (NIV)

34. Self-control is one of the most important things you can learn in life. If you can learn to not say things that are hurtful even when someone is being mean to you, or to not do something that everyone else is doing when you know it is wrong, or if you can make yourself wait for things when you really want them but it is not the time to have them, then you will be able to say "yes" to all that God has planned for your life. His plans aren't just "good", they are "the best"! When we can say "no" to things that would rob us of God's best, we will have an abundance of the Fruit of the Spirit growing in our lives.

Producing Good Fruit

....We ask God to give you complete knowledge of His will and to give you spiritual wisdom and understanding. Then the way you live will always honor and please the Lord, and your lives will produce every kind of good fruit. All the while, you will grow as you learn to know God better and better.

Col 1:9b-10 (NLT)

35. Pray every day that Jesus will show you who He is. Ask God for wisdom and faith. Read the Bible every day to see how you can be more like Him. Memorize Bible verses so that you won't disobey God. The more fruit you grow, the more you will bring honor to Jesus.

e|LIVE

listen|imagine|view|experience

AUDIO BOOK DOWNLOAD INCLUDED WITH THIS BOOK!

In your hands you hold a complete digital entertainment package. In addition to the paper version, you receive a free download of the audio version of this book. Simply use the code listed below when visiting our website. Once downloaded to your computer, you can listen to the book through your computer's speakers, burn it to an audio CD or save the file to your portable music device (such as Apple's popular iPod) and listen on the go!

How to get your free audio book digital download:

1. Visit www.tatepublishing.com and click on the e|LIVE logo on the home page.
2. Enter the following coupon code:
   bd9f-7409-b953-0574-e0ca-5884-67f0-a37a
3. Download the audio book from your e|LIVE digital locker and begin enjoying your new digital entertainment package today!